Music Minus One Clarinet

Buddy DeFranco

and You

3285

mmo

Buddy DeFranco

CONTENTS

ISBN 978-1-941566-17-6

WAVE

ANTONIO CARLOS JOBIM

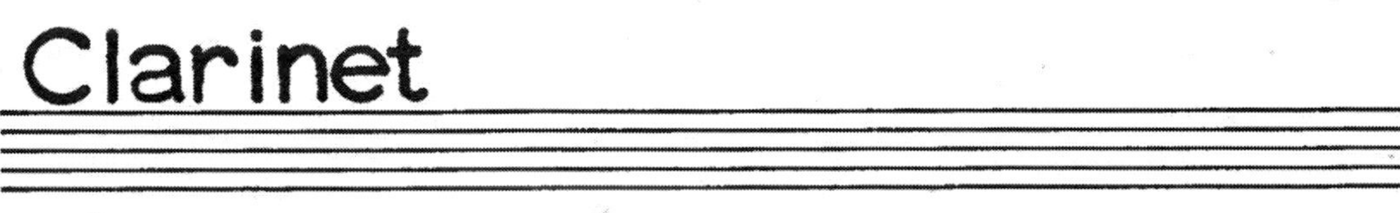

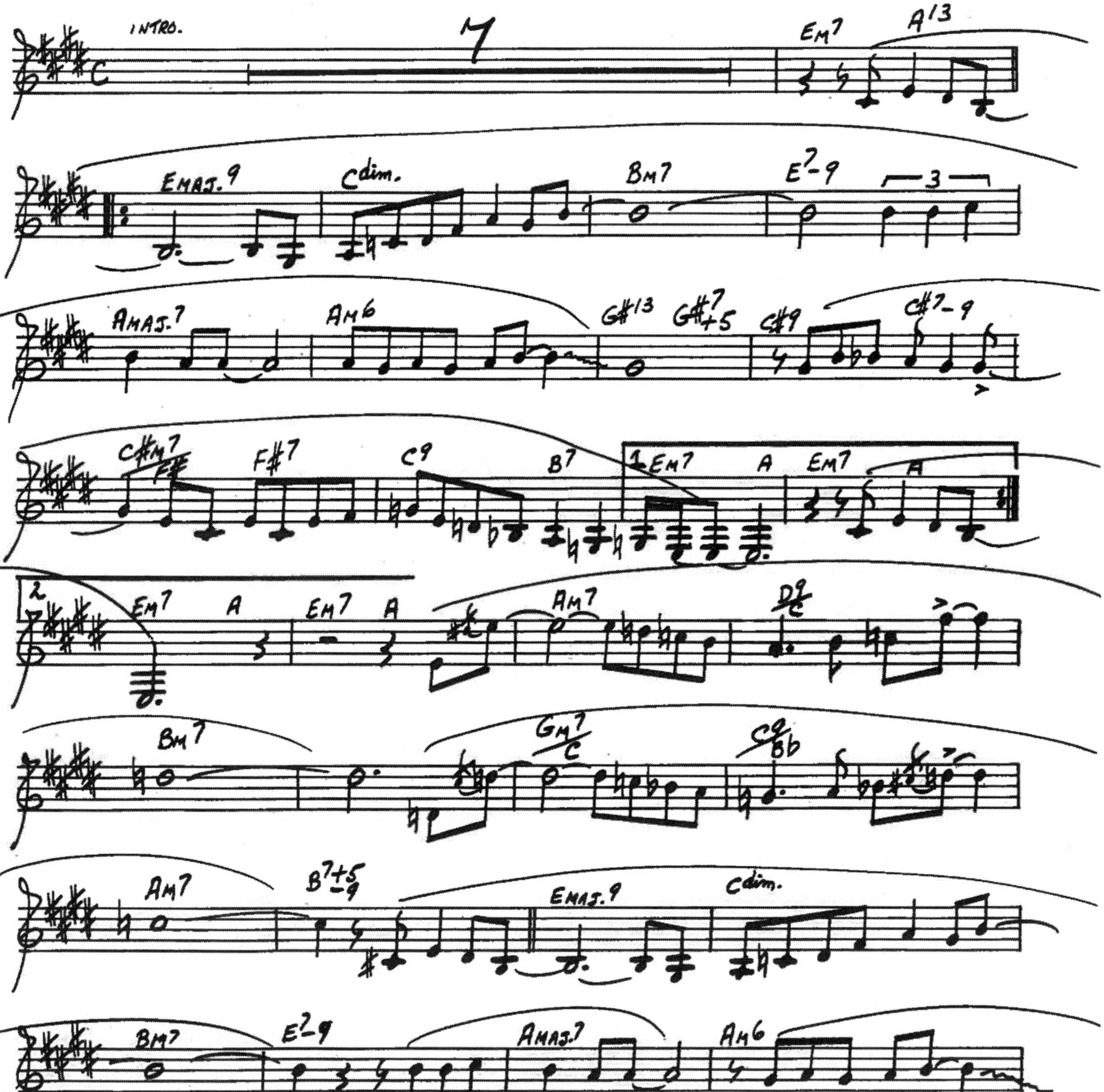

BOSSA NOVA

INTRO.

CLAR.-SOLO

EM7
A7
EM7
A7
(BRIDGE)
AM7
D13 9
G
G
GM7
C13 9
F
B+
EMAJ.7
Cdim.
BM7
E7+9
AMAJ.7
D13+11
C9
C#7
F#M7
C7-9
B7+9
EM7
A7
EM7
A7
EM7

PIANO & GUITAR
3
EMAJ.9
Cdim.
Bm7
AMAJ.7
Am6
G#13
C#9
F#7
C9
B7
Em7
A
Em7
A
Em7
A
fade

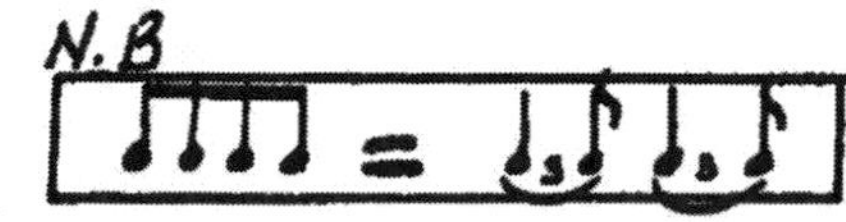

EASY

COMP./ARR. BUDDY DEFRANCO

Clarinet

TO CODA

CLAR. SOLO
Fm7
Fm7
Eb
Ab7+11
Eb
Gm7-5
Fm7
Ab7
EbMAJ.7
F#m7
B7
Fm7
Ab7
EbMAJ.7
C7-9
Fm7
C7-9
Fm7
Eb
Ab7+11
Eb
Ebm
Abm7
Db7
Eb

D.S. To CODA
CODA

BLUE POLY

COMP./ARR. BUDDY DEFRANCO

Clarinet

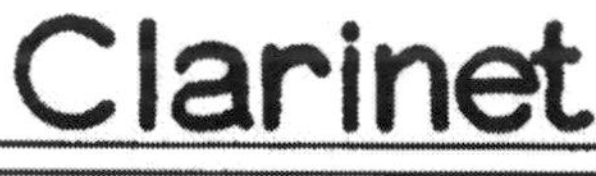

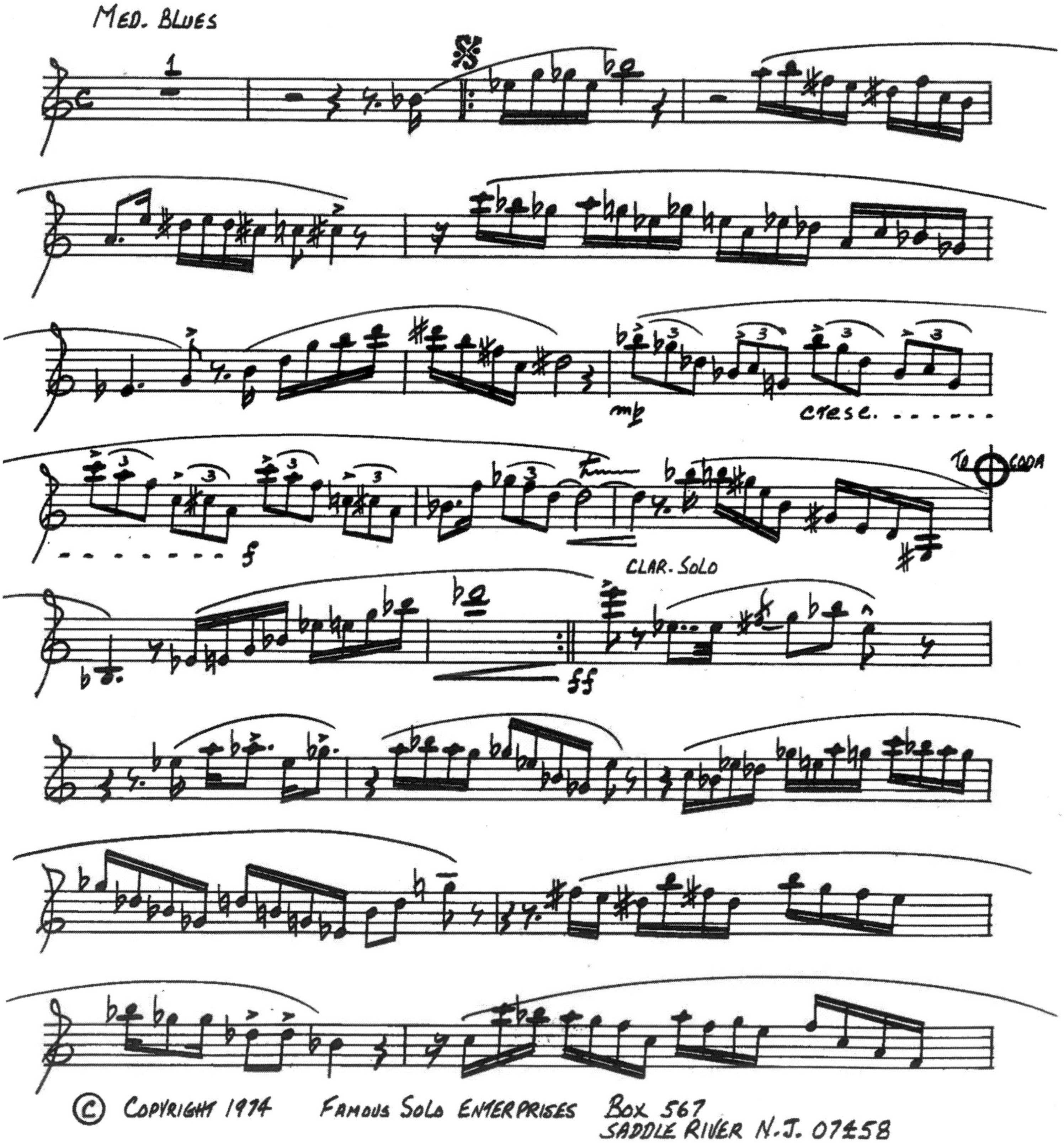
MED. BLUES
1
mp
cresc. . . . . . .
. . . . f
TO CODA
CLAR. SOLO
ff

GUITAR SOLO
12
11
D.S. TO CODA
CODA
fine

N. B.

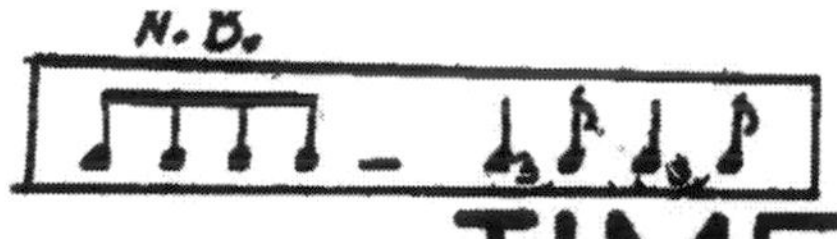

TIME DUST GATHERED

COMP. ROLAND HANNA

Clarinet

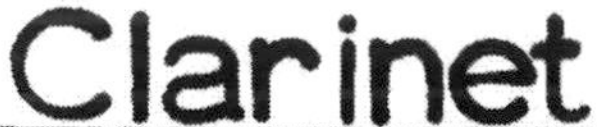

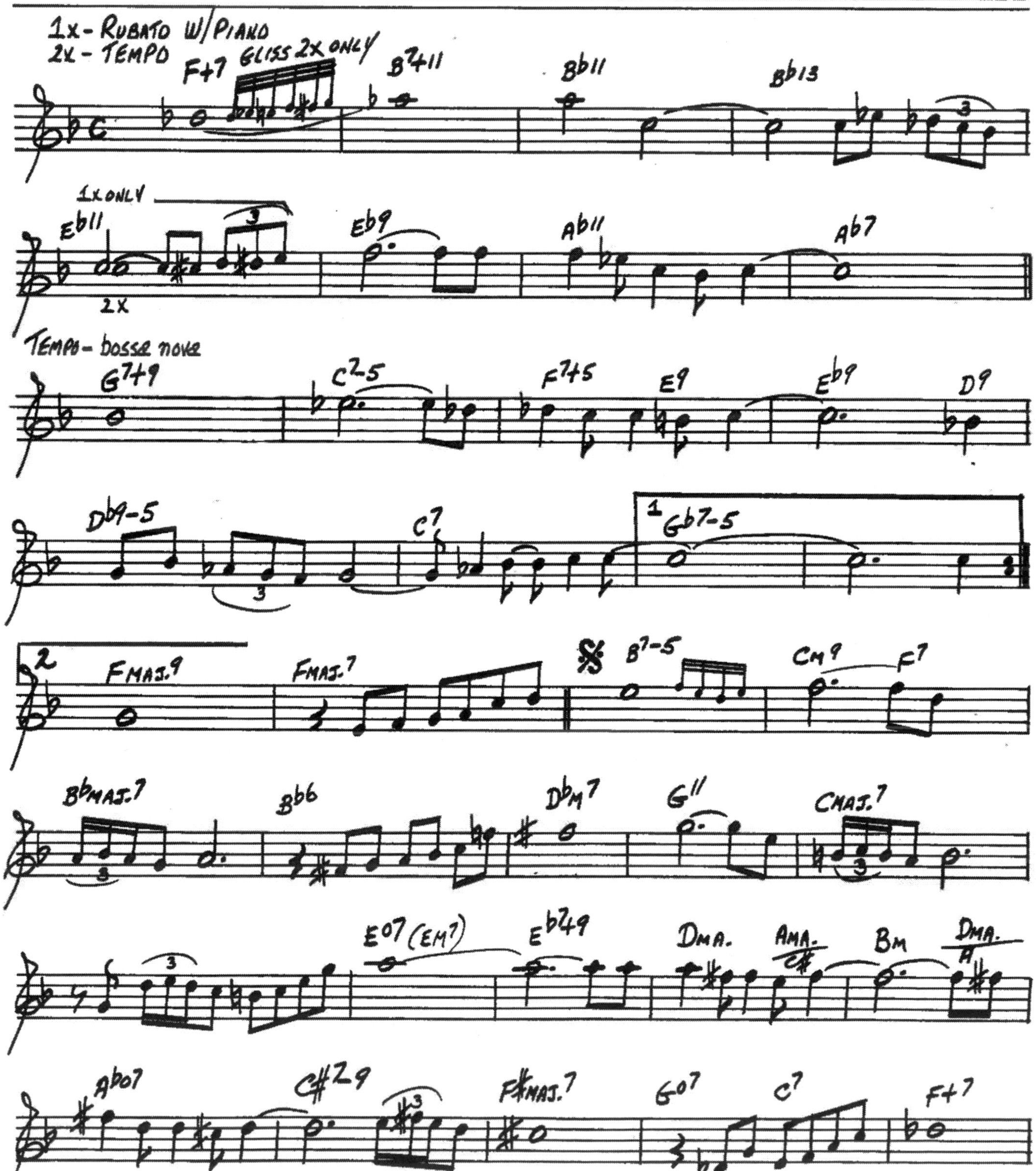

1x - RUBATO W/PIANO
2x - TEMPO
F+7
GLISS 2X ONLY
Bb7#11
Bb11
Bb13
1X ONLY
2X
Eb11
Eb9
Ab11
Ab7
TEMPO - bossa nova
G7+9
C7-5
F7+5
E9
Eb9
D9
Db9-5
C7
1
Gb7-5
2
FMAJ.9
FMAJ.7
B7-5
Cm9
F7
BbMAJ.7
Bb6
DbM7
G11
CMAJ.7
E07 (EM7)
Eb7+9
DMA.
AMA. / C#
Bm
DMA. / A
Ab07
C#7+9
F#MAJ.7
G07
C7
F+7

Bb7
Bb11
Bb13
Eb11
Eb9
Ab11
Ab7
G7+9
C7-5
F7+5
E9
Eb9
C9
Db9-5
C7
TO CODA
Gb7-5
CLAR SOLO
F7+9 b13
B7+11
Bb13+11
Eb
Eb13
Ab11
Ab7+11
G7+9
C7+9
F7
E7
Eb7
D7-9
Db9-5
C7
Gb7-5
Gb7-5
F7+9 -13
B7+11

Bb13+11
Eb11
Eb13
Ab11
Ab13
C7+9
F7
E7
Eb7
D7-9
Db9-5
C7-5
FMA.
B7-5
CM7
F7
BbMA.
Bb
DbM7
G11
CMA.
CMA.
EM7-5

A13
Eb7
DMA.
BM7
BM7
AbM7-5
C#7-9
F#MA.
Db+
F+
B7+11
Bb13+11
Bb13+11
Eb11
Eb9
Ab11
Ab7+11
G7+9
C7+9
F7
E7
Eb7
D7
Db9-5
Gb7-5
C7-5
Gb7-5
PIANO SOLO
15
(CLAR.)
D.S. TO CODA
CODA
PLAY TWICE
FADE

OUR STREET

COMP./ARR. BUDDY DE FRANCO

SLOW

TO CODA

CLAR. PLAYS 2 BARS FOR 1 BAR FOR RHYTHM
CLAR ♩ = ♪ RHYTHM
CLAR SOLO
A13
AM7
D7-9
GMAJ.7
BM7-5
E7+9
A13+11
A13+11
D13
D13
DM7
DM7
G7+9
G7+9
CMAJ.7
CMAJ.7
F9
F9
GMAJ.7
GMAJ.7
BM7

E7+9
A13+11
A13+11
F9
F9
Am7
D13-9
GMAJ7
1
D. S. To CODA
CODA
RIT.
fine

TOO CUTE

ROLAND HANNA

Clarinet

2 CLAR SOLO

Music Minus One
50 Executive Boulevard ▪ Elmsford, New York 10523-1325
914-592-1188 ▪ e-mail: info@musicminusone.com
www.musicminusone.com

ISBN 978-1-941566-17-6